EXTREME SURVIVAL

EXTREME SURVIVAL

Abbie Rushton

Collins

Contents

 **Your survival toolkit**

Super survivors are always prepared!
See what essentials you'd need to pack
in your rucksack:

food

water cleaning tablets

water bottle

map

compass

torch

first-aid kit

emergency blanket

tarp

3

 # Sensible survival tips

✓ Don't go anywhere without an adult.

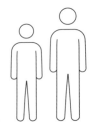

✓ Tell another adult exactly where you're going and when you will be back.

✓ Check the adult's mobile phone is charged up.

Wear the right gear.

CHAPTER 1
Survival in a forest

Introduction

You'd never want to be in a situation where you were fighting for survival. However, if you did need to keep yourself safe, would you know what to do?

This book will give you some ideas that might help you, and some stories of real survivors.

In this chapter, you'll learn about surviving in a forest. You'll discover how to build shelters, find water and steer clear of insects and animals that could seriously harm you.

Build a shelter

First, decide where to build your shelter.
Look for natural features like a cave,
fallen tree or overhanging rock.
But check that it's safe first and that
nothing can fall on you.

You should avoid:
- wet ground
- high ground, like hilltops
- low ground, like valleys or **ravines**
- bumpy or uneven ground
- ground next to a river.

Survival tip

The most important thing
to remember in any survival
situation is: don't panic!

If you have a tarpaulin (tarp) and some rope, find two trees about 3 metres apart. Then tie the tarp to them to make a tent shape:

tarp

If you only have branches and leaves, you can lean the branches against something. This could be a fallen tree or a large rock. Alternatively, you could put a long branch between two trees, like this:

The Science of survival

To keep warm, you need to stop heat leaving your shelter. You need some **insulation**. Use anything you can find to trap warm air inside. This might include:

- dead leaves
- moss
- smaller twigs
- mud.

Lay these over the branches, filling as many gaps as possible. Put some dead leaves on the ground to make a bed.

Find water

You might think that food is your next **priority**. However, humans can survive weeks without food. Without water, people can only survive for days.

Warning!

Any water that you find outside hasn't been cleaned. This includes running water in streams and rain water. It could contain **bacteria** or other substances that might make you poorly. Only drink water you find in the wild if you absolutely have to. Clean it first.

You can collect rain water with any containers you have. Or tie a tarp to some trees. Then place a rock in the middle to make a dip where water will collect.

Alternatively, pinch some water from plants! Tie a bag around a leafy plant. Leave it all day and water will appear in the bag.

The science of survival

Plants **absorb** water from soil. Any water that the plant doesn't need is released from the leaves. This is called transpiration.

Clean the water

Use what you have in your toolkit to clean the water. Ideally, you will have water cleaning tablets. The tablets contain a chemical that kills bacteria or anything else that might harm you. Always check the instructions when using these tablets.

If you don't have tablets and have no other option, boil the water and let it cool before drinking.

Know which insects and animals to avoid

There are a number of animals that should be avoided in a rainforest.

The Brazilian wandering spider is one of the deadliest known spiders. It's called a "wandering spider" because it wanders around on the forest floor in the day, so people need to watch where they're walking!

Some people think
that poison dart frogs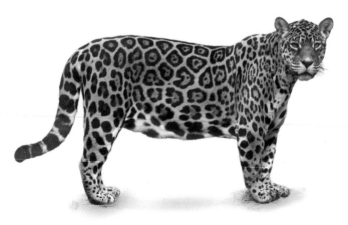
are the deadliest animals on Earth.
They are pretty, but their bright colours
are to warn other animals – including
humans – to stay away.

Jaguars don't eat humans, but they
might attack if frightened, and they are
killing machines! They would have no
problem attacking something as vicious
as an alligator.

Speaking of alligators ... you wouldn't want to come across one! Black caimans are the biggest alligator. Their dark colouring means they can easily hide in mud.

Another creature that hangs out on muddy riverbanks is the green anaconda – the heaviest snake in the world. There's no evidence that a green anaconda has ever eaten a human. However, scientists say that a green anaconda *could* eat a human, so we should all be careful!

Diary of a survivor

In 1971, a 17-year-old girl survived a three-kilometre fall after a plane crash in the Amazon rainforest.

Here is an extract from her diary:

When I woke up after the crash, I could hear planes searching overhead. I knew there wasn't much hope of them finding me. The forest was dense, and I couldn't even see the sky.

There wasn't much to eat because it was the wet season. There was hardly any fruit on the trees. Luckily, I found some sweets from the plane.

I was so grateful to my parents for everything they taught me when we lived in the rainforest. I knew from the sounds of the frogs and birds that I was in the same jungle we called home.

I found a small river and floated in that because I knew it would be safer. I went in the middle of the river because my father had taught me that dangerous fish preferred the shallow water.

After ten days, the teenager found a fishermen's hut. The next day, she was discovered and rescued by the fishermen.

CHAPTER 2
Survival at sea

Introduction

Lots of us like swimming in the sea, but you need to respect that the sea is a force of nature. It is unpredictable, so things can quickly go wrong.

You should do everything you can to avoid dangerous situations at sea. However, if you did end up stuck in a rip current, or lost at sea in a boat, you'd want to be prepared.

Survive without a boat

You shouldn't swim in deep water. However, if you find yourself in deep water and you're struggling, don't panic. Seize anything floating nearby. Raise your hand and try to get someone's attention.

If there's nothing to grab onto, the best way to save energy is to try to relax, lean back and float. Shout for help.

One of the biggest dangers of sea swimming are rip currents. These are narrow, fast-moving **channels** of water that move away from the shore.

Did you know?

Rip currents can move at about eight kilometres per hour. That's faster than an Olympic swimmer!

First, know how to spot a rip current. Look for patches of water that:

- are dark and foamy
- have no breaking waves
- are brown because of churned-up sand.

Can you spot the rip current here?

The Science of survival

Rip currents often form around a sandbar, which is a raised area of sand in the sea.

The waves travel over the top of the sandbar. When they move back again, they can't go back over the sandbar – only through small gaps in the sandbar.

The waves travel very fast because they are all squeezing through a small gap. This means there's a danger they might carry boats or swimmers out to sea.

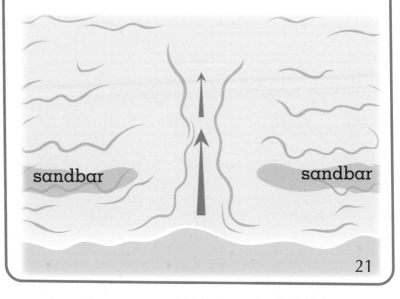

sandbar   sandbar

The biggest danger is that people panic when they are caught in a rip current. They use too much energy trying to swim back to shore. This exhausts them because they're swimming against the current. Trust me: it is a fight they will not win!

If you are caught in a rip current, swim sideways, following the shore.

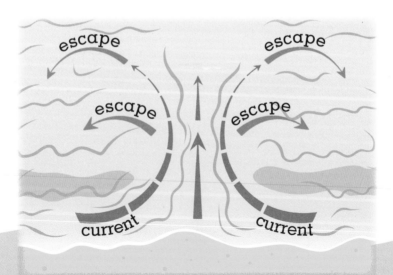

Survive with a boat

If someone was in the worst situation and they were lost at sea, the first rule is: Do not drink seawater! The salt in seawater will speed up dehydration.

The Science of survival

Water helps our bodies stay at the right temperature and get rid of waste. Dehydration is when someone's body doesn't have enough water to work properly. **Symptoms** include dizziness, headache and feeling weak.

Being lost at sea can be scary, even if you have a boat. How can you find your way back?

Sailors have used the stars to guide them for thousands of years. Different stars are used in different parts of the world.

There is an imaginary line called the equator around the middle of the world. Anything above the equator is called the northern hemisphere. Anything below it is called the southern hemisphere.

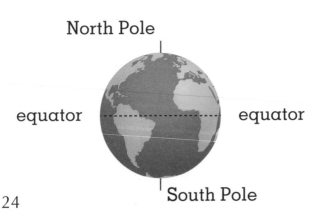

North Pole

equator

equator

South Pole

If someone were in the northern hemisphere, they'd need to find the North Star. This would help them know which way north was. The North Star always stays in the same place, above the North Pole.

First, they'd need to find the star pattern called the Big Dipper. It looks a bit like a cooking pot with a long handle. The two stars on the end of the "pot" point to the North Star.

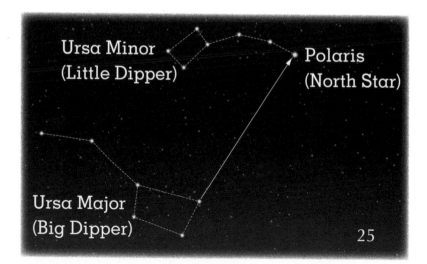

Ursa Minor
(Little Dipper)

Polaris
(North Star)

Ursa Major
(Big Dipper)

Similarly, if someone were in
the southern hemisphere, they'd need to
find the Southern Cross constellation to
know which way south was.

As well as trying to navigate to shore, it's important to signal for help. At night, you could flash a torch. Use this code: three short flashes, three long flashes, then three short flashes. If people see this, they will know someone is in trouble.

In the day, try using a mirror or something reflective to create a flash to get someone's attention. Or make a flag out of anything that's brightly coloured.

Man lost at sea for 24 days survived on ketchup

In December 2022, a man called Elvis was repairing his boat on the island of Saint Martin in the Caribbean. When a strong current swept his boat out to sea, Elvis tried to use his mobile phone to call for help, but there was no signal.

Incredibly, Elvis survived for almost a month on a bottle of tomato ketchup.

Eventually, Elvis used a mirror to signal a plane, and he was rescued by the Colombian navy.

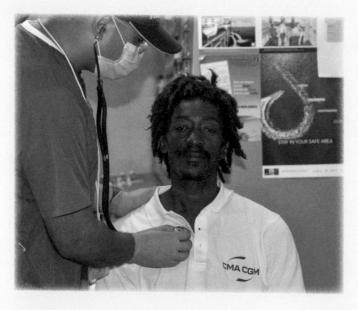

When a well-known ketchup
manufacturer heard about the story,
they started a campaign to find Elvis,
called "Find the Ketchup Boat Guy".
Thanks to the internet, the ketchup
manufacturer made contact with Elvis
and offered to give him a new boat!

Chapter 3
Survival in a desert

Introduction

You would not want to get lost
in a desert. Deserts are places of
extreme temperatures – often very
hot in the day and very cold at night.
They don't get much rain, and not much
grows there. This makes them a serious
survival challenge!

There are techniques you can learn
to protect yourself from danger.
These would help you if the worst did
happen and you were lost in a desert.

Protect yourself from the sun

Obviously, you should stay out of the sun as much as possible to avoid sunburn and heat exhaustion. You might find some shade created by sand dunes or large rocks.

Unlike in a forest, there won't be many materials around to build a shelter. If you have a tarpaulin or sheet, stretch it out between rocks.

Otherwise, look for a cave, but be careful – something else might be hiding in there!

Try to find shelter on high ground. You wouldn't want to be on low ground if there were a rain storm.

You might not expect to see a rain storm in a desert, but it does happen. The problem is that, when it rains heavily, the land is too dry to absorb the rain. So the rain could cascade downhill and sweep someone away.

Did you know?

More people drown in deserts than die of thirst.

The heat might make people want to lie down, but sand can be blisteringly hot! It's best for someone to raise themselves away from the sand by sitting on clothes or a bag.

If someone needed to walk somewhere, they should go after sunset, when it's cooler. But they shouldn't wait too long as temperatures can drop to below freezing at night.

Save sweat and find water

You can still become dehydrated, even with water available, if you sweat too much. So do as little as possible, especially during the day.

Survival tip

You might have heard that you can drink the liquid inside cacti. In fact, this is not true. The liquid is very acidic and would probably upset your stomach.

Save sweat, not water.

34

Use these things as your guides to find water:

- birds circling or flying insects

- plants growing

- low ground at the bottom of mountains.

Wait until night, then go to one of these areas and dig about 30 centimetres down. If the sand is damp, widen the hole. Wait a few hours for the hole to fill with water.

Survival tip

Remember to always clean any water before drinking it.

If you found plants, you might be able to collect dew (water droplets) from them early in the morning. You could use a cloth to soak it up.

You might find water in tree hollows or beneath rocks.

Remember, if you tie a bag around a leafy plant and leave it all day, water will collect in the bag.

Avoid deadly desert animals

Perhaps one of the most terrifying desert creatures is the scorpion. Desert scorpions are the largest in North America. They hide in caves during the day and come out at night, so watch out!

The tarantula hawk is neither a spider, nor a bird. It's a wasp which is supposed to have one of the most painful stings in the world.

This creature is the largest lizard in the United States. Most lizards are not **venomous**, but this one is. A bite from it wouldn't kill you, but it would make you seriously poorly.

Ostriches might look funny, but being kicked by an ostrich is no laughing matter. They can cause serious injuries if they feel their eggs are being threatened.

The cougar, or mountain lion, is a brilliant jumper. It's also very fast and good at climbing. If you meet a cougar, do not run. Make eye contact, as it will consider this a threat and leave.

Desert horned vipers are snakes with two horns made from modified scales above their eyes. They spend their days resting, often **concealed** in the sand, so it may be easy to tread on one accidentally.

CHAPTER 4
Surviving the cold

Introduction

Playing in the snow is lots of fun.
However, being stuck outside in freezing
temperatures with no shelter can
be life-threatening.

Discover some survival tips for extreme
cold, such as making a shelter, what
clothes to wear, and what to do in
a blizzard.

Build a shelter

If someone was stuck in the snow without a tent, they should make a snow cave.

The Science of survival

You learnt earlier that trapped air stops heat from escaping. Surprisingly, snow is a good insulator because it has pockets of air in it.

Step 1: Find the right spot. Look for snow that's about 1.5 metres deep. Snow on a short slope is ideal, but avoid larger slopes with lots of snow above as the snow could fall.

Step 2: Pack down the snow by stomping on it. Loose, powdery snow may crumble or collapse.

Step 3: Dig an entrance tunnel upwards into the slope. It should be a dome shape that's slightly wider and taller than the person.

Survival tip

Make your snow cave as small as possible. You should only just fit in. Larger shelters are harder to keep warm.

Step 4: Dig upwards to make a sleeping area. Dig the ceiling first, in another dome shape. If the walls or floor are dug first, the **structure** might collapse.

The Science of survival

Because heat rises, the sleeping area will be warmer and the cold air will stay in the entrance tunnel.

Step 5: Make the walls about 30 centimetres thick.

Step 6: Make sure there's air to breathe. Add air vents by poking holes through the walls with a stick or a shovel handle. Leave something poking out of the top of the snow cave to help you find it. The last thing you'd want after all this hard work is to miss it!

When it's time to sleep, put some insulation like leaves or branches beneath you. Never sleep directly on the snow.

Use your clothing

Aim to wear three loose layers.

The space between them will trap heat.

You should wear:

1. a base layer to
   absorb sweat
   from your body

2. a fleece layer
   for warmth

3. a waterproof
   layer to protect
   you from wind,
   rain and snow.

Survival tip

We release heat from any part of our body that isn't covered. So wear a hat. Choose one with ear flaps because frostbite (damage to your skin) is common on ears.

If you start to sweat when digging your snow cave, remove a layer. Damp clothes will make you colder.

Surprisingly, the advice if your clothes get very wet is to get naked! Your body will be able to control your temperature more easily than if you have wet clothes clinging to you.

Survival tip

The early stage of frostbite is called "frostnip".
Symptoms include: a tingling feeling, throbbing or aching.

45

Beating a blizzard

A blizzard is a severe snowstorm with high winds. The wind is a real danger because it blasts ice onto people, which melts on their skin and then refreezes.

The science of survival

Wind can cool down our bodies. This is called "wind chill". It happens when the wind blows warm air away from our bodies, reducing our overall temperature.

People can quickly become lost in a blizzard, as the swirling snow can really reduce visibility. If you were caught outside in a blizzard, the best thing would be not to walk too far.

Try to work out which way the wind is coming from, then find a nearby rock or tree. Shelter on the other side of that, so it protects you.

If possible, take shelter in a snow cave. Try to stay warm and **hydrated**.

You might think the best source of water is all around you: snow! However, you must not eat frozen snow as it will rapidly bring your temperature down. It can even make you more dehydrated, because of the work your body needs to do to heat and melt the snow.

 **Top tips for surviving in Antarctica**

Tip 1

Eat lots!

Eating helps to warm you up from the inside, and you will use a lot of energy walking through the snow.

Tip 2

Drink lots of water! You get through about three times as much water as usual, because the air is so dry.

Tip 3

Wear snowshoes.
They are bigger than
normal shoes so
it's easier to
walk in snow.

Tip 4

Test the ice
for cracks before
you tread on it.

Chapter 5
Storm survival

Introduction

There's more than one kind of storm. Storms can include heavy rain, strong winds, thunder and lightning. They can all be dangerous!

You shouldn't go out in any kind of storm. However, if you did experience a storm, there are lots of ways to stay safe.

How to handle hurricanes

Hurricanes (also known as typhoons or cyclones) are tropical storms. That means that they only form over warm seas.

The science of survival

The warm air above the sea rises. Other air is sucked in, and that air becomes warm too. This starts a **cycle** of storm clouds forming, and these clouds start to spin.

Hurricanes have wind speeds of at least 119 kilometres per hour.

Stay indoors during a hurricane. Stay away from windows and glass doors. Hide in a windowless room, like a large storeroom or hallway, or hide in a cellar or basement.

Never go outside until the hurricane has passed.

If the wind dies down and the sky above is clear of rain or clouds, be careful! It might seem like the hurricane has passed, but you could be in the eye of the storm. This is a small circle in the middle of the hurricane.

eye of the storm

Did you know?

In the southern hemisphere, hurricanes spin **clockwise**. In the northern hemisphere, hurricanes spin **anticlockwise**.

You might think that winds are the biggest danger in a hurricane, but actually, it's more likely to be fast-flowing water or storm surges. If you're told to leave your house because of the risk of these, you must do so at once.

Survive storm surges and fast-flowing water

Storm surges are rises in the sea level due to storms. They can cause damage on land, too. Storm surges can last for a few hours or even weeks, and they can affect inland rivers and streams, too.

Storm surges are very hard to predict. They depend on things like the speed the storm is travelling, and the shape of the coast.

This unpredictability makes them very dangerous!

If there is any risk of rising water levels near your home, you must get to higher ground straight away.

Survival tip

If the area is already underwater, do not walk through the water. It would only take 15 centimetres of moving water to knock you over. You can use a stick to check how deep the water is and how firm the ground is.

If you are swept away by water, use this technique:

1. Turn onto your back.
2. Point your feet upstream. This means the water should be flowing towards you.
3. Use your legs to push away any obstacles heading in your direction.
4. Look for something you can hold onto, like a tree branch.
5. Grab it and then move your feet to point downstream instead.
6. Shout for help.

Deal with dust and sandstorms

Dust and sandstorms happen in very dry places when strong winds lift sand or dust into the air.

If you're outside and see a dust or sandstorm coming, try to find shelter. Look for something like a large rock or a parked vehicle.

You need to stay there and not move. You won't be able to see much when the storm arrives so you can easily get lost.

If you can't find shelter, try to get to high ground. It may sound strange in high winds, but most of the dust or sand will be close to the ground. That means the air will be clearer higher up.

You should be wary of large flying objects. Crouch down low to the ground and protect yourself with a bag or your hands.

Wet some cloth and tie it around your mouth and nose. This will stop sand or dust from getting into your lungs. Put another piece of cloth around your eyes.

Survival tip

Sandstorms often happen at the same time as thunderstorms, so be aware of lightning strikes. Don't go to higher ground if there is lightning flashing around you.

Chapter 6
Surviving earthquakes

Introduction

Earthquakes are caused by underground rocks shifting. This makes the earth shake suddenly and often violently.

Some places have more earthquakes than others. This is because they're in areas where the massive underground rocks meet, and they rub together.

You should stay where you are when an earthquake strikes, whether that's indoors or outdoors. Find out how to survive both situations, and deal with what might happen afterwards.

Earthquake survival if you're indoors

If you have a warning that an earthquake is coming, make sure you open doors that go outside. This will stop them from getting stuck, so you still have a way out.

Move away from glass windows and doors and large pieces of furniture that might fall.

Drop, Cover, Hold on.

Drop means drop to the floor on your hands and knees. This will stop you hurting yourself if you fall.

Cover means hide under a solid piece of furniture, like a table or desk. Or go to an interior corner – one that's not near a window.

Hold on means hold on tight to the table or desk.

Survival tip

It is not recommended that you shelter in doorways because they won't protect you from falling objects.

Protect your head, with your hands or a pillow. If there's lots of dust, try to cover your mouth with a cloth.

Stay where you are until the shaking has stopped. Wait 1–2 minutes. Even when you think it's safe to move, be really careful. Most earthquakes have aftershocks, which are smaller quakes, but can still be very dangerous.

Earthquake survival if you're outdoors

The first thing to remember if you're outdoors during an earthquake is to move away from anything which might fall on you. This includes:

- buildings
- bridges
- tall trees
- streetlights and telephone poles.

Survival tip

Your instinct will probably be to seek shelter, but do not go under a bridge as it may collapse. You're safer out in the open.

Crouch down low to the ground. If you can find anything to cover your head, use it. This might be a rucksack or even a rubbish bin lid!

After the earthquake has finished, there may be a number of hazards outside, so watch out! There may be sinkholes, which are holes in the ground. There may be fallen trees, rubble or glass on the ground.

Surviving after an earthquake

If the shaking lasted more than 20 seconds, this could affect the sea. There is a high risk of a giant wave forming. So, if you live near the sea, you need to get to higher ground at once!

Did you know?

These giant waves may travel at up to 800 kilometres an hour. That's about as fast as a jet plane!

You need to move quickly. If you're indoors and can't get out, move to the highest floor of the building, or the roof if possible.

If you're outdoors, get as far inland as possible, on the highest ground you can find. If you don't have time, climb a tall tree and hold on tightly.

Another risk after an earthquake is a landslide. This is a sudden movement of rock and earth down a slope.

People can't outrun a landslide. They should try to move out of its path. If that's not possible, they should curl up into a ball and protect their head.

If someone is inside during a landslide, they should move as high up in the house as possible.

Did you know?

People who are on an upper floor, attic or roof in a landslide are 12 times more likely to survive.

A super survivor

Now you have the techniques to survive in a number of different dangerous situations.

Can you remember the most important thing in any survival situation?
Don't panic. If you breathe deeply and try to calm down, you will be able to practise what you've learnt. This might save your life, and other people's lives.

You are a super extreme survivor!

Glossary

absorb soak up liquid

anticlockwise the other direction to the way a clock's hands move

bacteria very small living things that can cause disease

channels places where water can move

clockwise the direction that a clock's hands move

concealed hidden

cycle when events happen repeatedly in the same order

hydrated having enough water

insulation something that stops heat from escaping

priority the most important thing to do

ravines valleys

structure something that's been built

symptoms things that show that your body isn't well

venomous containing poisons made by animals like snakes and spiders

Index

About the author

How did you get into writing?

It started off with a love
of storytelling. I used to tell
myself stories all the time – in
the swimming pool, on the way
to school, playing in the garden.
I'm sure I had a few strange looks
as I wandered around talking
to myself! My first piece of writing
was published at the age of nine.

Abbie Rushton

It's a wonderful feeling. It still feels special every time I see
my work in print.

**What do you hope readers will get out of
the book?**

Hopefully no one will ever be in a situation where they
need the advice in this book, but if they are and remember
what they've read, it might help to save them.

What is it like for you to write?

It can be the best feeling in the world! The ideas flow out
of me, the words arrange themselves in perfect sentences,
and occasionally they even sound good! But sometimes
it's painfully slow, I can't find the right words and I need
a lot of help to edit them so I make sense.

Is there anything in this book that relates to your own experiences?

Well, there was the time I wrestled an alligator, and stared down a mountain lion … only joking! I *wish* my life were that exciting! We don't have many alligators in England.

What is a book you remember loving reading when you were young? Why?

I Capture the Castle by Dodie Smith. Because it has the best opening line of any book ever, and I wish I'd written it! "I write this sitting in the kitchen sink."

Have you ever been in a tricky survival-type situation outdoors? What happened?

I've been on lots of adventures around the world, but I've never been in a serious survival situation. I'm so glad I wrote this book as I feel far more prepared!

What's your number-one tip for anyone preparing for an outdoors adventure?

Oooh, probably sensible shoes! The older I get, the more I care about sensible shoes! Don't get some fancy brand-new shoes and wear them for the first time on your adventure – they will probably rub against your skin and give you nasty blisters. Wear your comfiest, oldest shoes, as long as they're not full of holes!

Book chat

Which part of
the book did you
like best, and why?

What was the most
interesting thing you
learnt from reading
the book?

If you had to give
the book a new
title, what would
you choose?

Did you know any
of these survival
tips before reading
the book?

If you could interview one of the survivors who would you choose? What would you ask them?

What do you think is the most useful survival tip?

Which part of the book stands out most for you? Why?

What sort of environment would you like to explore? Why?

If you could ask
the author one question,
what would it be?

Have you
ever been in a
survival-type
situation?

Do you have
any of your own
survival tips you
could share?

Have you heard of
any other real-life
survival stories?

Why do you think this book is called *Extreme Survival*?

If you could give the author one piece of advice to improve the book, what would it be?

Would you recommend this book to a friend? Why or why not?

Book challenge: Make a list of things you would take on a trip.

Collins
BIG CAT

Published by Collins
An imprint of HarperCollinsPublishers
The News Building
1 London Bridge Street
London SE1 9GF
UK

Macken House
39/40 Mayor Street Upper
Dublin 1
D01 C9W8
Ireland

10 9 8 7 6 5 4 3 2

ISBN 978-0-00-862471-2

British Library Cataloguing-in-Publication
Data

A catalogue record for this publication is
available from the British Library.

Download the teaching notes and
word cards to accompany this book at:
http://littlewandle.org.uk/signupfluency/

Get the latest Collins Big Cat news at
collins.co.uk/collinsbigcat

Author: Abbie Rushton
Publisher: Lizzie Catford
Product manager: Caroline Green
Series editor: Charlotte Raby
Development editor: Catherine Baker
Commissioning editor: Suzannah Ditchburn
Project manager: Emily Hooton
Content editor: Daniela Mora Chavarría
Phonics reviewer: Rachel Russ
Copyeditor: Catherine Dakin
Proofreader: Gaynor Spry
Typesetter: 2Hoots Publishing Services Ltd
Cover designer: Emily Hooton
Production controller: Katharine Willard

Collins would like to thank the teachers and children at the
following schools who took part in the trialling of Big Cat
for Little Wandle Fluency: Burley And Woodhead Church
of England Primary School; Chesterton Primary School;
Lady Margaret Primary School; Little Sutton Primary School;
Parsloes Primary School.

Printed and bound in the UK by Page Bros Group Ltd

Acknowledgements
The publishers gratefully acknowledge the permission
granted to reproduce the copyright material in this book.
Every effort has been made to trace copyright holders and
to obtain their permission for the use of copyright material.
The publishers will gladly receive any information enabling
them to rectify any error or omission at the first opportunity.

Front cover: t Nynke van Holten/Shutterstock, bl
Giftography/Shutterstock, br Ernie Cooper/Shutterstock;
back cover: tl Anton Starikov/Shutterstock, tr Audrius
Merfeldas/Shutterstock, bl Photo smile/Shutterstock,
bc TheFarAwayKingdom/Shutterstock, br Eric Isselee/
Shutterstock

p3t Ionescu Bogdan Cristian/Alamy Stock Photo, p5b Peter
Cade/Getty Images, p8b Maksim Safaniuk/Alamy
Stock Photo, p10 Antonio Guillem/Alamy Stock Photo,
p12 Cordelia Molloy/Science Photo Library, p17b Associated
Press/Alamy Stock Photo, p19 John Wreford/istockphoto,
p27 NB/ROD/Alamy Stock Photo, p29 Associated Press/
Alamy Stock Photo, p33 Bashar Shglila/Getty Images,
p40 Imgorthand/Getty Images, p42 Alex Ratson/Getty
Images, p50 Ashley Cooper/Getty Images, p63 Ian
Davidson/Alamy Stock Photo, all other photos Shutterstock.

MIX
Paper | Supporting
responsible forestry
FSC
www.fsc.org
FSC™ C007454